C000163775

A Calvary Covenant

The Stations of the Cross

John Cullen

First published in 2020 by Messenger Publications

The material in this publication is protected by copyright law.
Except as may be permitted by law, no part of the material may be
reproduced (including by storage in a retrieval system) or transmitted in
any form or by any means, adapted, rented or lent without the written
permission of the copyright owners. Applications for permissions should
be addressed to the publisher.

The right of John Cullen to be identified as the
author of the Work has been asserted by him in accordance with the
Copyright and Related Rights Act, 2000.

ISBN: 9781788123105

Copyright © John Cullen, 2020

Scripture quotations are from several versions, including the New Revised
Standard Version which is used by permission.
All rights reserved worldwide.

Designed by Messenger Publications Design Department
Typeset in Plantin MT Pro and Luminari
Printed by Johnswood Press Limited
Cover image © Jacob_09 / Shutterstock

Messenger Publications,
37 Lower Place, Dublin D02 E5V0, Ireland
www.messenger.ie

This book
is dedicated to
The Sisters of Nazareth

Contents

Preface

Pause.
Pray.
Listen.
You have to stop,
to see and be still.

✳

We think we have to
catch up with the world.
Actually, we have to be still
to let the world catch up with us!

✳

You stand on the silent earth,
where all new life and creativity begins.
This is holy ground once more.

✳

It is here that the seed
you feared would die,
now breaks through.
A future never dreamed of
becomes possible.

God of the numbed ...
God who knows chaos ...
God who calls us *'Beloved'* ...
God of the frail in mind and body ...
God who feared to fracture ...
God who weeps ...

＊

God who watches through the night ...
God who creates in darkness ...
God who breathes life from dust ...

＊

Call us by name in this still space.
Awaken the faith and courage
we'd forgotten we had
as your parting gift to us.

Introduction

THESE words from Ben Sirach frame these reflections: 'The widow's tears run down the cheeks of God' (Sirach 35:18). This is not just an image, a metaphor or an allegory. God actually sheds tears and sweats blood for us all.

The Stations of the Cross trace deep emotions:
jealousy, betrayal, denial, cowardice, cruelty,
abandonment, mockery, shame, wickedness,
silence, suffering, steadfastness and sacrifice.
Jesus takes them all and more upon himself.

He is our God on his knees who washes feet.
He is our God who bites the dust.
He is our God who literally falls for us
so as to break all our falls and failures.

The Stations of the Cross invite us to
show one another the image of God
and grow in the likeness of Christ.

The Fourteen Stations are in the present tense.
What they say is happening now in your own life
or someone's life, somewhere in the world.

Background to the Stations of the Cross

THE earliest sources of the Stations of the Cross can be traced back to an account in the year 384. It is from a Spanish anchorite nun who reported the practice of people walking the Via Dolorosa, the path which Jesus carried the cross from the Praetorium in Pontius Pilate's palace to the hill of Golgotha.

The Crusaders, returning from the Holy Land, introduced the practice of the Stations of the Cross to Europe. This developed into the emergence of art works and paintings that elaborately depicted the important moments of Christ's journey being placed in churches.

Initially the depicted paintings numbered between five and forty-five. Over time the series of fourteen stations was established. Nine of the stations are mentioned in the Gospels from accounts relating to the passion of Jesus. The other five stations have their origin in stories and traditions that have been handed down over time.

Our Celtic High Crosses portray the story of Christ's suffering. They led people through this visual to pray and ponder the passion.

A fifteenth station has emerged in the twentieth century. It is the Resurrection. God lives where we let him love and lead us to life. On our pilgrim path as God's beloved and chosen people, may we recognise him and say, 'it is the Lord' (John 20:18).

The First Station
Jesus Is Condemned to Death

We adore you O Christ and we praise you.
Because by your Holy Cross you have redeemed the world.

Remember
✳

In this station we remember all those in authority.
'You would have no authority over me at all were it not
given to you from above' (John 19:11).

Meditation
✳

Pilate washes his hands, declaring his own innocence
before an innocent Jesus who stands before him.
Pilate sneaks his way into our third century creed
in the phrase about Jesus:
'For our sake he suffered under Pontius Pilate'.

We often use the phrase, 'my hands are tied'
to avoid responsibility or a difficult decision.
In this station God's hands are tied and bound.
God puts himself into our hands,
as Barabbas (meaning: son of the father) is released and
we join the baying chorus of the crowd who shriek out,
CRUCIFY HIM.

Be still
and Know
that I am God

Reflect
✳

'Man of sorrows wrapt in grief,
Lamb of love, our comfort be:
Hear our mournful litany.'
(#20 Hymn in the Divine Office, Volume 2)

Pray
✳

Our Father.

Sing
✳

'Be Still and Know that I Am God'
(Anonymous)

The Second Station
Jesus Takes Up His Cross

We adore you O Christ and we praise you.
Because by your Holy cross you have redeemed the world.

Remember
※

In this station we remember prisoners.
'I was in prison and you came to see me'
(Matthew 25:36).

Meditation
※

God created the heavens and the earth.
He saw all that he made and it was very good.
The air we breathe is God's gift to us.
We took the axe and laid it to the tree (Matthew 3:9).
We made a cross of all that God created
and gave it the one who set us free.

We tie heavy burdens on others shoulders
and do not lift a finger to help them (Matthew 23:4).
Sorrow now follows the experts in religious law
for depriving God's people of the gifts of his love
with harsh and cruel judgements.
We echo the words of Micah and T. S. Eliot:
'O my people what have I done unto thee'? (Micah 6:3)

I am the Lord that Healeth Thee

Reflect
*

'By the dire and deep distress
More than human mind can guess,
Lord, our grief in mercy see:
Hear our fervent litany.'
(#20 Hymn in the Divine Office, Volume 2)

Pray
*

Hail Mary ...

Sing
*

'I Am the Lord that Healeth Thee'
(Anonymous)

The Third Station
Jesus Falls the First Time

We adore you O Christ and we praise you.
Because by your Holy Cross you have redeemed the world.

Remember
✳
In this station we remember the homeless.

Meditation
✳

Here is the one who had nowhere to lay his head (Matthew 8:20).

He walks and stumbles along the stony path.

He is 'the stone rejected by the builders' (Matthew 21:42; Psalm 118:22).

The cheeky devil had asked Jesus to change stones into bread,

but Jesus 'lives on every word that comes from the mouth of God' (Matthew 4:3).

Jesus opts for the path of pain, passion and patience.
Here divinity bites the dust.
Humanity humiliated.
He sets his face like flint (Isaiah 50:7),
showing a stony resolve in the face of scorn.
He falls with us and for us that he
might break all our own
falls and failures.

In Thee
O Lord
I Put My Trust

Reflect
✳

'By that bitter cup of pain,
When your strength began to wane;
In your pity grant our plea,
Hear our solemn litany.'
(# 20 Hymn in the Divine Office, Volume 2)

Pray
✳

Glory be to the Father …

Sing
✳

'In Thee O Lord I Put My Trust'
(Anonymous)

The Fourth Station
Jesus Meets His Mother

We adore you O Christ and we praise you.
Because by your Holy Cross you have redeemed the world.

Remember
✳
In this station we remember all mothers.

Meditation
✳
'This Child is destined for the fall and rising of many,
a sign that will be contradicted' (Luke 2:34).
The encounter between Mother and Son
cannot be limited to paltry words.

In a world of wars, cruelty and human trafficking,
mothers follow dark paths to
cross unbearable thresholds of pain.
Mothers enfold our fractured world in a
heart-felt, embraced mantle of prayer.

Mary teaches us by her quiet example of discipleship
how to stay close to Jesus to the last.

O Lady,
full of God's
own grace

Reflect
✳

'By the cross's royal road,
Lead us to the throne of God,
There to sing triumphantly
Heaven's glorious litany.'
(#20 Hymn in the Divine Office Volume 2)

Pray
✳

The Memorare, 'Remember O Most Gracious Virgin Mary'

Sing
✳

Choose between:
'O Lady, full of God's own grace'
(composed by Estelle White)
'As I kneel before you'
(composed by Maria Parkinson)

The Fifth Station
Simon of Cyrene Helps Jesus to Carry His Cross

We adore you O Christ and we praise you.
Because by your Holy Cross you have redeemed the world.

Remember
✳

In this station we remember all the anonymous
people who help us.

Meditation
✳

'They compelled Simon of Cyrene to help Jesus carry the
   cross' (Luke 23:26).
As casual by-passers and bystanders,
we often turn away from the station of suffering.
The unforeseen is always possible.
Circumstances shape our lives.
We carry one another's crosses,
not by choice,
but by the chance accidents of life.

Simone of Cyrene,
the foreigner, the migrant, the outsider
is the patron saint of all those
who take up another's cross.
Simon is a dedicated person of
quiet service and calm deliberation.

Hail Redeemer King

Reflect
✳

'Oh, we have gladly heard your Word, your holy Word,
and now in answer, Lord, our gifts we bring.
Our selfish hearts make true, our failing faith renew,
our lives belong to you, our Lord and King.'
(Hymn: 'In Bread We Bring You Lord', composed by Kevin Nichols)

Pray
✳

Lamb of God, you take away the sins of the world …

Sing
✳

'Hail Redeemer King'
(composed by Patrick Brennan CSsR, 1877–1952)

The Sixth Station
Veronica Wipes the Face of Jesus

We adore you O Christ and we praise you.
Because by your Holy Cross you have redeemed the world.

Remember
✳
In this station we remember all the people
who quietly encourage us.

Meditation
✳

'As the crowd were appalled on seeing him
so disfigured did he look
that he seemed no longer human' (Isaiah 52:14).

Veronica saw someone different in the
spattered and battered face of Jesus.
She broke ranks to touch the
bruised face of God.
By her actions she embodies the words,
'In him is the invisible God' (Colossians 1:15).

Veronica is the true icon and servant
of hope and healing.
Her presence dispels the fears that
haunt and hurt human hearts.
Veronica creates a mobile laboratory of love.
She imitates the way Jesus taught by example,
to never throw in the towel.

Holy, Holy
Lord God
of Hosts

Reflect
✳

'Take all that daily toil, plant in our heart's poor soil,
take all we start and spoil each hopeful dream,
the chances we have missed, the graces we resist.
Lord, in thy Eucharist, take and redeem.'

(Hymn: 'In Bread We Bring You Lord', composed by Kevin Nichols)

Pray
✳

Support us Lord all day long …

Sing
✳

'Holy, Holy Lord God of Hosts …'

(written by Christopher Wordsworth, 1807–1885)

21

The Seventh Station
Jesus Falls the Second Time

We adore you O Christ and we praise you.
Because by you Holy Cross you have redeemed the world.

Remember
✳
In this station we remember displaced
migrants across the world.

Meditation
✳

'Do not neglect to show hospitality to strangers, for by doing that, some have entertained angels without knowing it' (Deuteronomy 10:19)

There is a new sculpture by Timothy Schmalz in St Peter's Square in Rome.
There are 140 migrants of various cultures and from historic times:
Jews fleeing the Nazis and Poles fleeing communism,
Syrians and Africans displaced by persecution, war, famine and poverty.

The 140 figures correspond to the 140 sculptures in the colonnades
of St Peter's Square, designed by Gian Lorenzo Bernini (1598–1680).
Four migrants from different countries and different religions unveiled this sculpture as Pope Francis blessed it.

This second fall of Jesus represents the globalisation of indifference that many migrants experience as victims of our throwaway culture.

Reflect
✳

Waste places of Jerusalem, break forth with joy!
We are redeemed, redeemed.
The Lord has saved and comforted his people
Our God reigns... Our God Reigns...
('Nearer My God To Thee' by Sarah Flower Adams)

Pray
✳

O Angel of God, my guardian dear …

Sing
✳

'Do not be afraid, for I have redeemed you.
I have called you by your name, you are mine.
When you dwell in the in exile of a stranger,
remember you are precious in my eyes.'
(composed by Gerald Markland)

*Do not are
be afraid*

The Eighth Station
Jesus Consoles the Women of Jerusalem

We adore you O Christ and we praise you.
Because by your Holy Cross you have redeemed the world.

Remember
✳

'Daughters of Jerusalem, weep not for me,
but for yourselves and for your children' (Luke 23:28).
In this station we remember all those who
cry aloud and silent tears.

Meditation
✳

'My tears have become my bread, by night and by day'
(Psalm 42:3).
Tears are a deeply personal expression of our feelings.
They serve as a powerful connection
between our thoughts and emotions.

Psalm 58:8 reminds us:
'You have kept a record of my tears.'
Isaiah etches for us an intimate and tender image of God:
'He will wipe away the tears from every cheek' (Isaiah
25:8).
These weeping women dare to
make a choice to create a space that
unites them with the suffering Christ.
They remain anonymous as the
Lord responds with compassion.

24

But you are always close to me

Reflect
❋

'Deep in thy Sacred Heart let me abide,
Thou who has come for me, suffered and died.
Sweet shall my weeping be, grief surely leading me,
Nearer my God to thee, Nearer to thee.'

Pray
❋

Deliver us Lord from every evil …

Sing
❋

'But you are always close to me
following all my ways.
May I be always close to you
following all your ways, Lord.'

('I watch the Sunrise', composed by John Glynn.)

The Ninth Station
Jesus Falls the Third Time

We adore you O Christ and we praise you.
Because by your Holy Cross you have redeemed the world.

Remember
✳

In this station we remember all who suffer
from any form of addiction.

Meditation
✳

'The young may grow tied and weary, they stumble and fall,
but all who put their hope in God renew their strength'
(Isaiah 40:30).

The Prophet Isaiah reminds us that though we may be tired,
God is never tired of us.

We may be trampling on God, wounding God, neglecting
God

ignoring God, forgetting God, insulting God.

But God keeps coming back to us,

despite the elaborate devices we construct to keep God
away.

Whatever you are, married, single, divorced, married again,
consecrated, ordained, in ministry, on a sabbatical,

God, without a trace of self-pity and with loving eyes,

meets us in our falls, failures and feckless forgetfulness

with the gracious gift of a forever forgiveness.

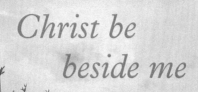

Christ be beside me

Reflect
✳

'We hold a treasure, not made of gold,
in earthen vessels, wealth untold;
one treasure only:
the Lord, the Christ in earthen vessels.'

('Earthen Vessels' by John Foley SJ)

Pray
✳

*Lord Jesus Christ, you said to your apostles,
'I leave you peace … my peace I leave you' …*

Sing
✳

'Christ be beside me, Christ be before me,
Christ be behind me, King of my heart.
Christ be within me, Christ be below me,
Christ be above me, never to part.'

(adapted from St Patrick's Breastplate by James Quinn SJ)

The Tenth Station
Jesus Is Stripped of His Garments

We adore you O Christ and we praise you.
Because by your Holy Cross you have redeemed the world.

Remember
✳

In this station we remember all
who are jobless and homeless.

Meditation
✳

'They divided my clothing among them.
They cast lots for my robe' (Matthew 27:35).
From swaddling clothes to a stripped off garment
that is diced in a game where 'lots' are bartered for his
  robe.
Jesus, once called the Bridegroom (Matthew 25:6)
endures further shame, reproach, derision and contempt.
Here, our degraded Lord honours, heals and holds all
whose bodily dignity is outraged and abused.
Here is God's covenant of grace sealed by his suffering.
No gilded throne, no weighty sceptre,
no intricate, dogmatic definition of the deposit of faith.
We have a Christ who is 'Hosanna in the lowest' all the
  way down to us.

Strength and protection may thy Passion be

Reflection
✳

'Stand and stare not at what used to be
and remain not in the past.
For I, says he, make new beginnings.
Look, all things are new, do you not see?'
(Huub Oosterhuis, Dutch Liturgist and Composer)

Pray
✳

*We proclaim your Death, O Lord, and profess your
resurrection until you come again.*

Sing
✳

'Strength and protection may thy Passion be;
O Blessed Jesus, hear and answer me;
deep in thy wounds Lord, hide and shelter me;
so shall I never, never part from thee.'
('Soul of My Saviour': Ascribed to Pope John XXII, 1249–1334)

The Eleventh Station
Jesus Is Nailed to the Cross

We adore you O Christ and we praise you.
Because by your Holy Cross you have redeemed the world.

Remember
✳

In this station we remember all those
affected by violence.

Meditation
✳

'Stretch out your hand over the sea and divide it,

that the people may go on dry ground through the sea'
   (Exodus 14:16).

St John's Gospel (6:67) records a story about the closest
   friends of Jesus

who reject him. They turn their backs on him.

He looks to his disciples and asks: 'Will you also go away?'

It is as if the future of the mission of Jesus hangs on this
   question.

Maybe even the future of Christianity rests in the balance.

St Peter is the one who answers:

'To whom shall we go? You have the words of eternal life.'

In the face of disappointment, destruction and devastation

we glimpse the aching and anguished face of God.

In this station, God's love is stretched to his finger-tips.

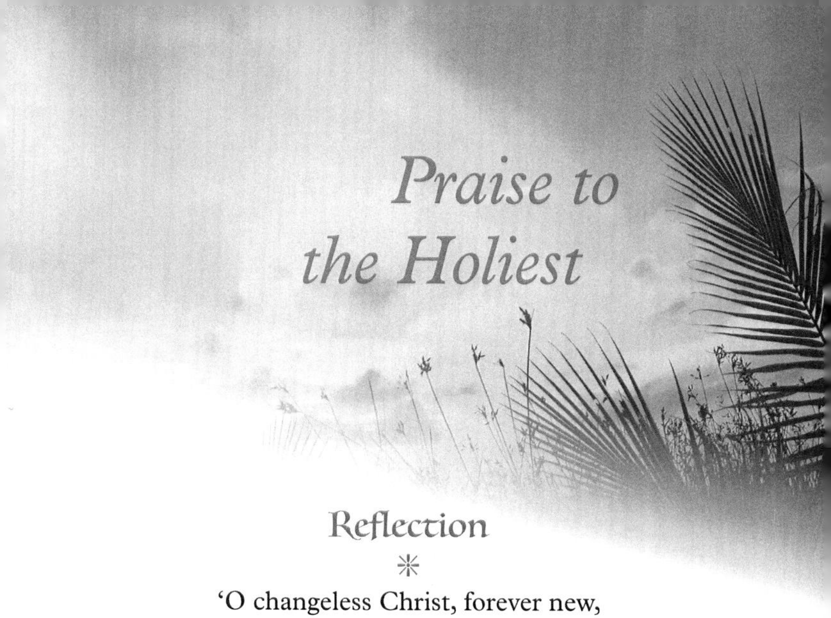

Praise to the Holiest

Reflection

✳

'O changeless Christ, forever new,
who walked our earthly ways,
still draw our hearts as once you drew
the hearts of other days.'

(composed by Timothy Dudley-Smith)

Pray

✳

Pour fourth we beseech thee O Lord, thy grace into our hearts.

Sing

✳

'And in the garden secretly
and on the Cross on high,
should teach his brethren and inspire
to suffer and to die.'

(Verse 5, 'Praise to the Holiest', by John Henry Newman, 1801–1890)

The Twelfth Station
Jesus Dies on the Cross

We adore you O Christ and we praise you.
Because by your Holy Cross you have redeemed the world.

Remember
✳
In this station we remember all our dead.

Meditation
✳
'You are dust and unto dust you will return' (Genesis 3:9)

The term 'Ground Zero' is associated with 11 September 2001.
But the term was first used during the 1945 bombing of Japan.
The fearsome weapons killed 200,000 civilians.
Ground Zero came to mean that part of the ground situated directly under the detonated bomb in Hiroshima and Nagasaki.

Look at the Genesis words: the dust of the earth, the dust of the desert,
the dust of trampled dreams, the dust of fire-ravaged bodies,
the dust of Auschwitz, Srebrenica, Phnom Penh, the dust of 9/11.

Today's gathering dust in war-torn Iraq, Syria, Yemen, Afghanistan,
the dust covering the mass-graves because of the coronavirus.
Gethsemane, Golgotha and Calvary were Ground Zero zones.
God started from zero and created something eternal.
Our hope is in God's promised whisper from the top of the Cross,★
'Today you will be with me in Paradise' (Luke 23:43).

Reflect
✳

'Thyself, dear Jesus, trace me
that passage to the grave.
And from thy cross embrace me
with arms outstretched to save.'
*(thirteenth-century hymn, # 23 Hymn, O Sacred Head ill-used,
Divine Office, Volume 2)*

Pray
✳

Eternal rest grant unto them O Lord …

Sing
✳

'Were you there when they crucified my Lord?'
(American spiritual, composed in 1899)

★*Ardnacrusha is a village in County Clare that is the location of the Electricity Power Base.
In Irish, Árd na Chroise means the top of the Cross. Since 1111, a Cross marks the boundary
between Killaloe and Limerick Dioceses.*

The Thirteenth Station
Jesus Is Taken Down from the Cross

We adore you O Christ and we praise you.
Because by your Holy Cross you have redeemed the world.

Remember
✳

In this station we remember helpers, carers and volunteers.

Meditation
✳

'He will be great and will be called the Son of the Most
  High' (Luke 1:32).

One night, in 1493, the young Michelangelo, aged only
  twenty-three,

broke into the Chapel of Santa Petronilla and chiselled
  into his first masterpiece the words,

'Michelangelo Buonarroti Florentine made this'

The masterpiece was the *Pietá*.

A rival sculptor, Cristoforo Salari threatened to claim it as
  his own work.

Michelangelo later regretted his outburst of pride and
  never again added a

personal signature to any of piece of his work.

The *Pietá* belongs to this station. It is the station of
  wordless tenderness.

It is the station of profound tragedy and sorrow.

It speaks of the heartbreak of mothers in every time and place.

During the COVID-19 pandemic, mothers, fathers, sons, daughters and closest friends

were not able to touch their loved ones in that final journey into death.

God is one of us who dwells among us and shares in our humanity.

Here is God who descends with us in the dereliction and agony of death.

Jesus is the light of our darkness, sent to illuminate our earthly night.

Reflection
✳

'Come back to me with all your heart.
Don't let fear keep us apart.
Trees do bend, though straight and tall;
so must we to other's call.'
(composed by Gregory Norbet OSB)

Pray
✳

Blessed be the name of Jesus, blessed be his holy name.

Sing
✳

'Jesus, remember me when you come
into your kingdom …'
(Taizé Chant)

The Fourteenth Station
Jesus Is Placed in the Tomb

We adore you O Christ and we praise you.
Because by your Holy Cross you have redeemed the world.

Remember
✳

In this station we remember all who are
on a journey of mourning and grief.

Meditation
✳

'O where can I go from your spirit? If I lie in the grave you
are there' (Psalm 138).

Women anoint the body of Jesus, soothing his scarred
flesh with tenderness.

Mary of Bethany had started a 'revolution of tenderness'
in the house of Simon the Leper,

when she anointed the feet of Jesus in preparation for his
burial.

In the Apostles Creed we recite that Jesus 'descended into
hell'.

The Eastern Orthodox traditions call Holy Saturday,
Silent Saturday.

Christ, the New Adam descends into the underworld,

calling out as he did in the Garden of Eden, 'Where are
you?'

We all have our own underworld, our personal hell.

At this station, Christ is like a pearl seeker,

as he is described in the Syrian tradition, he searches our dark depths

for the lost wonder and beauty of God's created image in us.

He takes us by the hand to shepherd us home, back to the fold,

into the heart of God's eternal love.

Reflect
✳

'Shepherd me O God
Beyond my wants
Beyond my fears
From death into life.'
(composed by Marty Haugen)

Pray
✳

Jesus, Mary and Joseph, I give you my heart and my soul …

Sing
✳

'How Great Thou Art'
(Composed by Carl Boberg, 1850–1940)

Afterword

The accounts of the Resurrection tell us about a running
   race
between Peter and John to the tomb.
Running is part of the Resurrection story!
Mary Magdalene is asked to 'Go and tell'
the frightened disciples the news that the Lord has risen.

St Paul uses a phrase:
'We have the mind of Christ' (1 Corinthians 2:16).
St Paul doesn't say:

> We have seen it;
> We have heard it;
> We read it somewhere;
> We need to think about it;
> We had an assembly about it;
> We have a diocesan plan about it;
> We will get around to it one day;
> We respect it;
> We admire it;
> We love it as an idea for going forward;

Paul tells us: *we have the mind of Christ.*

This is the Church's test in the face of

> new technologies,
> environmental challenges,
> political turbulence,
> faith on the frontiers,
> faith at the peripheries,

faith in the overwhelming knowledge we possess,
faith in all the contradictory experiences we meet,
faith in the endless choices we are offered,
faith in the debates about ministry.

Am I denying that I have truly been given
the mind of Christ?

'On the third day he rose again' *(The Apostles Creed)*

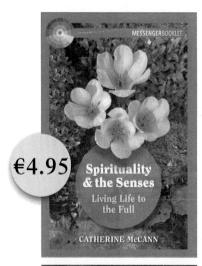

MESSENGERBOOKLET

Spirituality & the Senses

Living Life to the Full

CATHERINE McCANN

€4.95

The Sacred Heart Messenger

Pedro Arrupe SJ

BRIAN GROGAN SJ

M

€4.9

The Sacred Heart Messenger

FINDING GOD in a LEAF

THE MYSTICISM OF *LAUDATO SI'*

BRIAN GROGAN SJ

A MONTH OF REFLECTIONS

M

€4.95

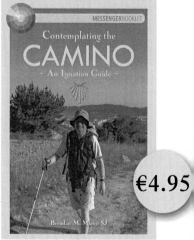

MESSENGERBOOKLET

Contemplating the **CAMINO**

~ An Ignatian Guide ~

Brendan McManus SJ

€4.95

www.messenger.ie